Away with the Fairies

CONFESSIONS OF A CLAIRVOYANT &
HOW TO COMMUNICATE WITH *SPIRIT*

"Is there a dimension beyond the Earth Plane? Is it real? Are we part of one great universe containing human beings and spirit beings?

Is there an invisible world that can be tapped into by certain gifted people? Can we communicate with the spirit world?

Effervescent Clairvoyant, Psychic and Medium, Pam Bradbury has 'tuned in' to other dimensions thousands of times as people come to her for clairvoyant readings. In this light-hearted book, you will gain and insight into her work.

Some of her stories are risqué, some deeply tinged with emotion. All of them are fascinating. Each of them has a message.

There is a higher dimension that Pam taps into. This book allows you to share the experience".

Ian Ward
Perth, Western Australia

Away with the Fairies

CONFESSIONS OF A CLAIRVOYANT &
HOW TO COMMUNICATE WITH *SPIRIT*
Written by Pam Bradbury

ABOUT THE AUTHOR

Pam Bradbury was born in 1948 in North Wales. She started her working life as a High School teacher in London. Her husband Colin created their first overseas adventure by moving the family to Hong Kong in the Seventies. That was a brilliant idea, beginning Pam's awakening, and has never been the same since.

In 1980 the family moved to Australia, the land of the Dreamtime. Australia and its wide-open spaces helped to further open Pam's mind to understanding and developing her clairvoyant and medium gifts. There is still much to learn and Pam knows that with maturity, even more will be revealed to her.

Pam's philosophy is to learn to live your life the way you dream. More and more people are living intuitively and creatively. Pam encourages everyone she meets to Step Up, Step Out and Dare. Change is healthy and brings with it; self-growth.

Acknowledgements

This little book is written from the heart.

Life is an adventure if you allow it to be. What lies ahead and in the future is mostly created by your past. To all those dear friends who have encouraged and supported me in this field of endeavour I say thank you from the bottom of my heart.

To have people in my life who believe in me is an added bonus. To Colin, Ellie, Ruth and Nick – my 'family', thank you for listening and being there for me. Sometimes I know I bored you to sleep.

To my spirit guides, whoever you are, stay with me, I love you all.

Published and distributed by Pen Publishing
Typesetting by Linkletters, Subiaco, Western Australia
ISBN 0958673608

Away with the Fairies

CONFESSIONS OF A CLAIRVOYANT &
HOW TO COMMUNICATE WITH *SPIRIT*

For my best friend and husband Colin. Thank you for always supporting me in all my endeavours. Keep smiling, there's a miracle on the way!

Contents

Away with the Fairies

You're a clairvoyant you know! The cards tell me that, in fact you are a medium! Hasn't anyone told you before?

"No", I said in a weak voice. "This is the first time I've visited someone like you."

"Well you are, it's a gift and not one to be abused. Within two years you'll be channeling information yourself."

Ugh, I thought visualizing myself cross legged on the floor, listening to wailing dolphins and dreary New Age music. Not my scene, I'd come to hear about being rich and famous, with my first best-seller.

"Can't you see anything about my book? It's a story about my Granny Sylvia," I asked pleadingly.

"No", he interrupted, "there's nothing here about your writing ability, but I can see a Chinese gentleman standing right next to you, shaking his head. He wants you to know that he's your guide."

Oh God, not the Chinese guide routine. I was nervous. I began to think that this bloke had lost the plot. But, can this guide guru tell me about my book then?

"Sorry love, no book".

His long slim fingers pointing to the cards.

Each card looked menacing to me, horrid colours and evil looking faces. He continued, "You live out of the city in the hills, you have three children, one is a Gemini. I thought, Gawd, she sounds like a car.

"You have a daughter who is a singer and your son has lady luck on his side. Your husband has been overseas and had just returned, he will go away again soon."

Yes, I knew all that.

"Your problem is you're bored. The answer lies in the cards, start channeling, that will sort it out."

He scribbled something on a card and handed it to me with the advice to visit this lady as she would 'open me up'.

I imagined myself gut open, hanging on the butcher's hook, innards exposed to the whole world. That did it, I had had enough. I just wanted to get out of the place as fast as I could. The incense was making me feel sick and the awful piped music was mournful.

I like music with guts, not this bland, drift-off stuff. I'm passionate. Besides he hadn't even told me what I wanted to hear. I stood to go.

"Must go, gotta get the kids from school…must go, must dash," I said "see ya." I dropped the obligatory fee on the table and stumbled out the door.

Bugger! Bugger! Bugger! Why didn't he tell me about my book? I know it's good. Oh Granny, does this mean I have to give you up? All that work and those hilarious true stories. Oh my heart hurts.

Now what do I do with myself? I can't be a clairvoyant. Those people always wear flowing robes, have long hair and look like relics from the sixties. As for being a medium, 'they' sit and talk to dead people all day, they're really 'away with the fairies'.

Just imagine bringing back my mouldy lot of relatives, that weirdo Aunt with all the cats and her dreadful hats, she was a health hazard and a liability. Heaven forbid, and Uncle Charlie with his Guinness and hand rolled fag, hanging from the corner of his mouth.

As I remember it, he died broke and we had to pay for his funeral. I really can't imagine what good it would be, contacting those two. They were of little use when living, so what possible help can they be dead?

However, if there was one relative who was wealthy and had hidden some money somewhere, that would be a darn good contact. But no, that's not possible as I know they were all broke.

No, I'm not going to be a medium either. That's not for me and anyway, there's no money in that business. If I'm not going to be a famous author, I might as well have a shot at being rich. I really need some money right now.

There's only one thing to do, it's time to say a few 'Hail Mary's, Jesus, Mary and Joseph and all the blessed saints, do something. It's a real shame I'm not a Catholic, but you never know, God just might be listening! If so, please could you send me a miracle!

Sadly, I put the book away and shut the door on my dream – I answered an advertisement for a sales rep's position. I hadn't sold a thing in my life, however blind faith and masses of enthusiasm helped and I also managed to create a very healthy bank account. It seemed my prayers had been answered as I was on my way to being rich.

However, I had this gnawing feeling in my stomach that something was missing. I had forgotten about the essential miracle. There was no passion in what I was doing. It was a means to an end.

This robotic existence had to stop, things had to change. I remember sitting alone one evening, day dreaming and calling up my beloved blessed saints, 'Come on Guys, it's time to help out.'

As I sat there steadily sinking into oblivion with the help of a glass of Chardonnay, the name Roma came filtering through.

Roma! Roma? At first, all I could think of was coffee. Perhaps I needed a coffee, and then it hit me, that card the Tarot man had given me last year. Roma that was the name he had written.

As luck had it, I found the card, dialed the number, held my breath, counted to twenty five and with a dry throat, asked for Roma. Yes, she was a Medium. Yes, I could join one of her closed circles; luckily she had just one spare place!

All I could think of was people sitting in the dark with their eyes closed, all holding hands and asking "Is anyone there?" I was frightened, I felt as if I was abseiling off a cliff, blindfold.

What if one of my dead relatives comes to haunt me, after all I wasn't very charitable towards them with my comments and I have always been scared of ghosts. I tried to blank the thought of the mystic circle out of my mind and reassured myself that ghosts don't really exist.

Roma was a total surprise. She was a real lady, like an elegant swan with grace and dignity, her composure was self-assured and not at all the image I was expecting.

She worked as a secretary for a large mining company, definitely not 'away with the fairies'. I relaxed immediately. I felt safe; I knew I could trust this woman.

There were only four of us in the group and we were all new to this work. Fate and destiny were weaving their magic web as within half an hour of the first session, Roma had us all working together in harmony, with a synergy of higher consciousness.

The miracle I had asked for, was happening, I not only felt the essence of people who were existing 'on the other side', I could hear their voices. With gentleness and confidence, Roma helped each of us to accept this from the internal person, not the external environment. It was the most profound experience I have ever had.

An awakening was taking place within me and I was adjusting to the fact that I was also still normal, not 'away with the fairies'. Roma's passion became mine. I had found a mentor, my life changed. I had purpose and I had much to learn, experience and do.

Little did I realize at that point of time, the extent of the miracle which was unfolding before me. I'm still reeling from the shock!

Jean Pierre

Nineteen ninety was an amazing year. One of those magical years amidst a few boring, uneventful ones. I felt at times as if I had been pushed off a cliff and told "just fly".

It was all my eldest daughters' fault. She kept sending all her girlfriends to see me. I think she fancied the idea that her mum could tell fortunes. Even I was amazed, the information seemed to come out of the air. I wondered sometimes if it was me or not. It was quite unnerving. I can remember feeling cautious and terribly careful about what I said.

For quite a while, I did not understand what I was doing, I was so inexperienced. To me it was fun and exciting, especially when I got it right. Wow, but I did dread it every time my daughter brought a new girlfriend home. The poor victim had been primed up to expect a reading.

I would talk about everything under the sun to avoid the reason for the visit. Then my youngest daughter would casually walk out of the room and that was the cue. She'd drag big sister with her and I'd be left there with the 'friend'. It was a bit like going to the dentist.

This pattern continued for several months, and then one day I got the first phone call. It was someone we didn't know, some how my number had been passed around. The voice, asked if I could help her French boyfriend Jean Pierre, he was very special to her, but a little confused. He needed to know things. How could I refuse – the girl sounded so concerned? We fixed a day and a time. I didn't think to ask how old the boyfriend was.

Why do all French men smell different? It must be those Gitanes cigarettes they all smoke. I knew he was at the door even before the doorbell rang – I could smell him. Tall and suave with sex appeal that oozed out of every pore.

He was aware of his sexuality and proud of it. He was no boy, he was definitely a man. My heart thumped in my chest, I could hear it. How could I – a suburban housewife help this gorgeous French man? I opened the door.

"It is I, Jean Pierre, I have com' for ze reading. You are Pam, yes?"

I lost my voice. It sorted of squeezed out of me, a feeble… "Yes, I am Pam, do come in".

He followed me into my office. It seemed small. His energy filled the whole room. I did not know where to look at first, his face, his eyes, his hands. I focused on his hands. I asked him to sit down and began to explain the process of my work.

He was impatient and said "Yes, yes, we 'ave many clairvoyants in France, I 'ave been to many. My grandmother, she was psychic."

I felt the perspiration running under my arms and other places too! Oh, for a toy boy just like you, whoops, where did that come from? I'm almost old enough to be his mother. I started to compose myself. 'Keep calm Pam, keep calm.

Concentrate, focus, relax, and think nothing. Yes, think nothing. That's the key, and then Spirit can come and work through me. I must get Pam out of the way. Now shut up and clear off Pam! Ah! That's it, cleared'.

"Well I seem to have a horse with you – a large cart horse." In my head I am thinking, 'what the hell is all this about?'

"Yes! Yes! That is my 'orse, 'ees name is Jacques". (I thought. Wow, it's right).

"Can you see im? Is 'e alright? I 'ad to leave 'im on a farm in Port Augusta, I was so upset. 'E 'as been all around Australia with me."

"No, he's fine. There are other animals with him…they look like goats, with long legs."

"No, they are Lamas, it was ze lady, she 'as a Lama farm."

"Oh that explains the long legs". I said "What do you see next?" he asked.

"Oh, three ladies, one is very fat and has an apron on. Is this your mother? Has your mother been sick? She appears to be lying down."

"Yes my mother is ill. I had a letter from my sister to tell me to come soon."

"No, you do not have to go home until Christmas, then you must go quickly. You will leave Australia forever. I have another lady here. She is very cross and has papers in her hands and she is arguing with you. She wants you to pay her money for something. I can see a house, in its own grounds.

This lady has a younger daughter. The child is not yours. Is this correct?"

"Yes, yes, go on!" he pleaded. "The lady needs to talk to you. Do you owe her money Jean Pierre?"

"Yes, It's a big problem, that is why I 'av come to you. She is my wife but I do not want her. I love women Pam, I just have to love them all. I marry 'er so I can stay in Australia as a citizen. I think of 'er as my non-wife. The child is from another man."

"There is a third lady. She is crying and very lonely. Who is she?" I asked.

"Oh, you can see 'er 'air?" said Jean Pierre eagerly.

"It is long and red but not really red – it's burgundy. She is tiny, slim like a doll."

"Yes, zat's Danielle, she's my non-wife's sister, I love 'er too."

By this time I was about to ask how many he'd loved on the way from Port Augusta to Perth, but thought better of it.

"It is ze smell of women I love. They smell of ze earth to me!"

I thought, have I got the right earthy smell on? No, I was wearing Gardenia or some such flowery rubbish. Must remember to wear earthy perfume near these French men.

"Well, Jean Pierre, you have problems with these two women. You have to contact the one with the papers or she will do something nasty. These papers look serious.

They have stamps on them. I have a man here who is handing you an envelope. It looks like a summons. I feel frightened for you. Now I see you up North, on a rig.

You are lifting heavy things and there is an accident – it is not serious, it is only your foot. I see the foot in plaster."

"You are right, I'm going up to Port 'edland to work for one of the mining companies. Do I make much money?"

"Yes, there is money here, but the work will come to a quick end. Christmas is good but an odd time for you. You are not going to stay in Australia for very long."

"I do not like to hear zat news. I love this country, ze woman are so free and there are so many 'ungry, sexy women."

I had heard enough about his conquests by now to feel glad I was old enough to be his mother. The reading came to an end and I ushered him out the door. I did not expect to hear from Jean Pierre again. However, one week before Christmas, the phone rang…

"Pam, do you know who ziz is?"

"Of course, Jean Pierre." How could I forget that sultry French voice which no woman could resist?

"Pam I need to come and see you. I am at ze airport. I have five hours to wait for my flight to Sydney."

Within half an hour, Jean Pierre was at the door. He was laughing. "You are a good clairvoyant, 'ere look at my toe."

He explained that when he left me, he remembered to take care on the drilling rigs and always wore safety boots – he was determined to outwit fate. One night he went to help some friends organise a party. He was unloading some kegs of beer off the back of a ute when a keg dropped onto his bare foot and nearly severed his big right toe. He said it freaked him out.

Then last week, the non-wife found him and told him the immigration people wanted him to come for an interview so they could assess whether the marriage was legitimate.

The wife was not going to help him unless Jean Pierre bought the house she was in and paid all the bills. He also had a letter from his sister to say he must come home quickly, as his mother was seriously ill.

"What do I do Pammie? You must 'elp me. What can you see?"

"I see a mess all around you." You didn't have to be psychic to see that! "Well all I can say is that you will leave Australia and never return here."

"But what about Jacques my 'orse?"

"Say goodbye to him too, Jean Pierre, he's happy with the long legged goats."

"Oh, oh my Pammie, what 'as 'appened to me?"

"Sounds as if your ladies are calling all the shots. What about the other lady, the one called Danielle?"

"Oh 'er! She's gone off with the father of my non- wife's child."

"She will contest the immigration papers too. Sounds to me, you either pay the money or run."

"I think I 'ave decided to run. I get this plane to Sydney and the next flight to France. I be 'ome by Christmas – good eh, Pammie? You 'ave been so 'elpful."

"I can't see how – you made your own decision."

"But just to talk about it, is so good. I will say goodbye to you, 'ere is a present for you." Into my hand he placed a photo of himself. I still have it today and often take it out of my diary and wonder who Jean Pierre is seducing now.

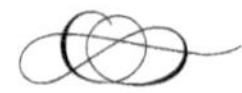

What's It All About?

I can remember thinking, 'Gaw'd this psychic stuff really does work. I must stop analysing the whys and wherefores of 'it' and just accept this skill'.

But the nagging question would not leave me, how, what and who gives me this information?

Is this really a gift? I must learn more. I started to take the work seriously in the hope I would gain more insight. As the months past I slowly realized...

Come In Swimmer

The sound of a person's voice over the telephone tells you so much, if you listen on a deep level. I have discovered it is possible to 'tune in' to people over the phone. I started to realise that several things were happening to me, on an internal level.

It was important to listen within myself, not to what the person was saying, rather to turn my head on one side, then listen carefully to my internal voice. It is a slow process at first as sometimes the internal voice is very faint.

Other times it is possible to hear one word really clearly, almost as if someone is shouting in your head. When you utter the first word, the rest just follows, without you knowing what you're going to say next. It is a weird concept; however I have now learnt to trust the information coming to me.

I have watched and witnessed peoples' stories unfold over many years with absolute incredulity at the turn of events. One such person was my dear friend Barbara. I met Barbara in February 1991 when she telephoned to make a booking for a reading.

There was urgency in her voice; she simply needed to see me that day, or as soon as possible.

I was receiving information about her over the telephone, I knew she was struggling with her emotions as I was hearing something about a really difficult relationship. When Barbara arrived at 5pm, straight from work, she was uptight, hot and anxious.

In those days I was using playing cards as a focus, to clear my own thoughts out of the way. I placed the cards out in front of her. It was not the cards that told the story, it was the voice within my head. I heard the words: 'arguments, one man, two women'.

"You are having an affair with a married man – correct?"

"Yes, I need to know the outcome. Please, what can you see?"

"It is not what I see, it is more what I hear. I am receiving information about a man who is a little overweight, with a frigid, icy wife."

"Yes that is correct."

"He will not leave this woman, it's his second marriage."

Her face dropped. This wasn't what she wanted to hear. She was dreaming of illicit weekends, snatched moments and romance, with the guy eventually leaving his wife for her. Real Mills and Boons stuff. "Sorry, it's not going to happen. Best you leave this relationship right now and start a new life."

"But, he tells me he loves me."

"He may do, in his own way."

"Bastard," she screamed. "Promises, promises – men are all the same, tell you anything to keep you sweet."

I went on to say, "Hey! Look, there are a few romances here, and in particular there is a new one on the horizon."

She relaxed and let me speak. "Oh! Quick, quick, tell me more."

"I have information about a man who loves water. He lives near the ocean, he is divorced, his children are adults. He must be a swimmer, he has a barrel-shaped chest." We both begin to giggle, Barbara's mood lightened, I continued.

"He is comfortably off. He enjoys all the things you like. His car makes a statement – it's large and maroon. He will think you are the 'ant's pants.' He is independent and likes his own space. He wants to shower you with poems and cards and small gifts."

"When, when will I meet him? Where? How? Who with?"

"Hey! I am not a magician" – I stumbled along trying to tune into the right month. "It feels like May to me, but please remember that time is not linear."

She didn't listen to that, she had heard all she wanted to know.

As she left, I knew I would see her again. I did not realise at the same time that Barbara would become a very close friend.

Within four months, Barbara was back in a terrible state of depression. The relationship with the married man had ended and she needed to talk about the new man, to get a clearer picture of him.

I had little to add, except reassurance and a box of tissues. Barbara kept in touch by telephone. Several months passed and her calls told me of dinner dates, outings and new adventures.

She was making progress and filling her life with new things. Then May arrived and disaster struck.

"But you said…" she muttered, when she rang to tell me all about 'Motor Mouth Mike', the new man in her life.

As she told me about Mike, my stomach turned over, I felt queasy. He didn't feel right. She had tried to fit him into the description I had given her. He didn't. He also had a wife who was a manic depressive and there was no way he was going to leave her. He was playing the field.

I wondered why a lovely lady like Barbara had such a complicated life. I kept my counsel as this affair became very nasty. Eventually, close to a breakdown, Barbara walked away from another disaster.

She pulled herself out of the depths of despair. She sold her house, moved to a new part of town, kept away from the clubs and dinner groups. She brought herself a dog and filled her life with wholesome things – her family.

Then one weekend she was asked to make up the numbers at a dinner party. She almost refused the invitation.

This time, it was the real Mills and Boons stuff. Steve first saw her, from across the room, the woman with the smile as big as the moon and the sparkly eyes. He knew she was for him!

He was a keen swimmer and lived near the ocean. His family were all grown up and he was divorced. It was love at first sight. Steve and Barbara has since become an 'item'. They have recently purchased a retail business as partners – their car is maroon! They are talking about a future together. They know their romance is special.

Life is full of surprises. If you leave it alone it all plays out as it should. The lesson is… "Know what you want, then sit back and let life bring it to you."

Hidden Gifts and Talents

Everyone possesses the faculty of clairvoyance, to a greater or lesser degree. With some people the psychic ability comes naturally and may first be experienced in childhood. With others, the faculty may need to be developed by training and this may take several years.

We keep the mystery alive when we talk about gifts from the gods. I suppose this is because we use words loosely and say things like, "Oh, that person is a gifted musician, or artist, or is a gifted public speaker."

It is time we opened our minds to this ability and cleared this old pattern of thought. People with a developed faculty of clairvoyance simply have an additional sense of perception.

It has nothing to do with our moral, ethical or religious teaching, any more than our eyesight depends on whether we are Catholic, Hindu, or Christian.

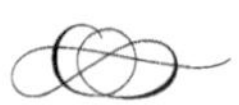

The Turning Point

Things were happening to me again on an internal level and at times, I didn't know how to cope, Roma had moved away and I felt very isolated. I had no-one to share my experience with. I lived through each emotion and worked through understanding the reasons later.

I remember one particular day when sadness swept over me in waves. I could not shift it, nor could I figure out the reason, it was just there engulfing me. I wanted to cry silently and quietly, all alone.

I could also smell perfume – light, watery perfume. The tears and the perfume haunted me all morning. I had a clairvoyant reading at 3pm, and I really needed to shift this mood. How could I work when I was engulfed in this melancholy?

At three o'clock Sandy arrived, her face was shadowed with sadness. Here stood a lady who was grieving; she was struggling with life's ups and downs with more than her share of sorrow. I said nothing and in my usual effervescent way, ushered her into my sanctuary.

Little did I know what was about to unfold and how my life would change, once again. This time it would be to a level of deeper understanding.

As soon as Sandy sat in the chair, a lady in a blue dress came forward in my mind. My stomach tightened I knew I was tapping into something that I had not experienced before. I froze. The image was ethereal.

I had heard people talk about visions, was this one? She looked real!

I heard a voice say, "Relax" and I remember letting go of my breath slowly and telling my body to relax.

It seemed to be an eternity before I spoke.

I could see her clearly now, she was very young, about twenty-three and dressed in a lovely, floaty, blue evening dress and she was smiling. She was so happy to be here. I wanted to cry for the joy of it, I could not stop the emotion.

What do I do now, I thought. I realised I had tapped into spirit energy. The lady in the blue must be a member of Sandy's family.

"Sandy, who is this young lady you have brought with you?"

Sandy turned in her chair to look. I smiled and said "No, it's alright – it is a Spirit person. She is young, tall and she feels like a sister."

I went on to describe her dress. Sandy told me her sister had died ten years ago. Sandy's composure dissolved with mine, emotion overwhelmed us both.

"She is so beautiful," was all I could say. The emotion I felt totally consumed me. I couldn't speak, the pain, the hurt within was like a dagger through my heart.

We sat in silence, the stillness and silence within the room was like a healing, as if someone had repaired a wound, closed a gap. It was eerie but so peaceful tranquility filled my body.

I realised it was the silence of death, of nothingness, which had a softness almost like the gentleness of the breath, of a sigh. Ah, so this is love, pure love.

I wanted to stay in this space where nothing mattered, nothing at all, then Sandy spoke first, her voice broke the silence.

"Yes, you are right. It is my sister. She was killed eleven years ago in a car accident on Greenmount Hill. She was so young, she had just got married, they were both so happy.

They were going to a ball, they had just left my house, she was wearing my blue dress. I had insisted she drive up to my place, borrow my dress, go to the ball from my home.

God, how I wish I hadn't done that, she'd be alive today. She died in the blue dress. Her husband was driving the car, it wasn't his fault, but he never got over the shock.

He has since remarried and can't bear to have anything to do with our family now."

"I want to call her Linda or Lillian is that correct?"

"No, it was 'Lizabeth."

We sat and held each others' hands for a moment. I then realised that 'Lizabeth had been trying to get through to me all day. Oh! The relief and the sense of understanding was electric.

My energy shifted, I spoke in such a rush I couldn't stop. The excitement was intense.

"Oh Sandy!" She has so much to say I must keep going – just hold my hands as I talk. She is telling me you have a small son, he is gorgeous and that you have had many miscarriages, that this boys is very special – a gift for you.

She tells me you help many people and that you have a dress shop. Is this correct?"

Sandy nodded; we both knew instinctively not to interrupt the flow of my words.

"She wants to talk about her bedroom. As girls you shared a room?" Another nod. "You had blue bedspreads, they matched?"

"Yes"

"You still have yours? She says take it out of the laundry cupboard and cut it up please, use it on your son's bed? She will be there at night and protect him, please do this for her."

"Your mother, let her hear this news. It will help her to realise that we never die, we go on forever into this infinity."

"Your sister is happy, so happy to be here. She wishes she could stay but her energy is fading. She says have fun with the dress shop, she loves the clothes you buy. She often comes with you in your car.

Don't keep the shop more than four years, you will sell it quickly. Your marriage is safe, all is well. Keep working with flowers and always live near the bush." She faded and was gone. I felt elated, alive, so alive. It was incredible feeling of lightness, as if I were floating on the ceiling. The sadness that had lingered with me had lifted. I realised it was Sandy's sadness, not her sisters.

We talked and I explained to Sandy that her sister had been with me all morning and that this was the first time I had experienced an overwhelming emotion being transmitted to me in this work.

Sandy said she had carried the guilt about her sister all these years and that this opportunity had helped her more than I could know. Now, she could let go, put the agony away and feel her sister's love and joy.

We spent more than half an hour sharing together what has happened for each of us and I can still recall Sandy's face as she left the house. A sense of peace was there that she did not have before and I felt that I could fly through the sky.

For the first time I realised the true significance of this work, the necessity to carry on and the real benefits to people. From that day on I have never questioned life after death. I know without a shadow of a doubt that we go on forever.

The spirit of this beautiful young woman had touched my heart, my own soul. She had opened me up as a person; Her spirit helped me to feel pure love, unconditional love.

I sat alone without moving for half an hour, marvelling at this experience. Then I wanted to scream and shout, to tell the world to come alive, to feel the joy and love of living.

The beautiful young woman in the blue dress was my first contact with Spirit Energy. This was a major turning point in my life and I am forever indebted to her.

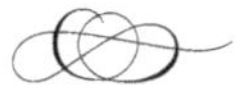

Big Jim

As I adjusted to the development of these internal senses, I found myself reverting back to good old prayer. I think I deserve to get an A, for prayer. It has to be my best subject. Whoever invented prayer came up with a damn fine idea.

I really don't know who I pray to, but pray I do. It has brought incredible miracles into my life and gives me a sense of relief and inner strength.

That there is a power greater than me I have no doubt whatsoever. What form and shape it has is of no consequence to me – just having a deep feeling of knowing is enough.

My religious education ended when my parents realised the local minister was gay. Up to that time, the family were regular churchgoers and my father was a deacon of the Church.

It seemed rather odd when all this fervent activity stopped abruptly. Being young and unaware of sexuality at that stage. I did not understand.

The idea of a God sitting on a throne doling out "Hell and Damnation" never really came into my consciousness. Nevertheless, I became a dab hand at prayer, especially when the requests came true. This childlike approach to God had never left me, I still pray like I am a ten-year-old.

I was uttering one of my biggest and best prayers when an enormous bronze Cadillac with menacing black windows crept down our potholed drive.

Everybody complained about our driveway, only the reckless actually attempted to drive down it, so when the Cadillac came to a halt, I knew someone either desperate or sinister was behind the wheel.

My senses were inclined towards the sinister and the "Hail Mary's" were rushing into my heart and head.

"Jesus, Mary and Joseph and all the Blessed Saints, who is this?"

Out stepped Jim, who was as wide as he was tall. All muscle and square, I froze inside. He was dressed in the traditional Aussie gear of black shorts, singlet and thongs.

The clothes I could cope with… it was his size, the Mohawk haircut and the tattoos that covered his face, arms and legs. All the flesh that was visible was painted tattoo black – that frightened me.

I prayed my best Grade-A prayer and remember saying to myself as I asked him into the house, 'If God (whoever he is) wants me to do this work, then God will protect me.'

I also remember thinking, "position him in the corner and sit next to the door." My mouth was dry. I grabbed the glass of water and thought 'OK God, over to you. Now what do I do?'

I took a deep breath and asked "Big" Jim if he worked on the fairgrounds, as I could see bumper cars and money belts and smelt mechanics grease.

He said he worked with go-karts in a travelling entertainment company. I tried to relax. This man was so uptight. He was like a wound-up spinning top, his insides were as rigid and hard as his outward appearance, how sad!

How could I get him to relax? I was back praying, 'God please help me, don't leave me, where are you? Spirit beloved Spirit, help, quick do something.'

Then Wham, Bang! Into the room in front of me, stood two huge warriors. I nearly fell off the chair, I was now sharing my tiny room with three men built like marauding mammoths, my knees shook and my jaw dropped.

'All the Blessed Saints, who are these people?' Gulping down my fear, I started.

"Jim, I have two men here, I think they are family members of yours, they look alike." He looked around, he started to shake. "It's alright," I said "They have come to talk to you through me. Let's find out who they are."

I took hold of his huge hand – to stop him shaking – it made mine look like a two-year-olds. I wanted to giggle but that was probably a reaction to my fear.

"Jim, one of them is holding a guitar and the other is giving me some boxing gloves. There is also a ship here – one of the men is talking and the other one is very quiet. They both look like Maori wrestlers or chieftains. They have come to give you all their love, one says he is John and is the other your Dad?"

At this point Big Jim broke down. He couldn't hold back his emotions any longer. He sobbed and sobbed for what seemed an eternity. It was obvious that he hadn't cried for a very long time – if ever.

I let him cry. I sat in silence. " My soul and heart reached out to him, I could feel his pain. He sobbed for himself, his life, his pain. He stopped and looked into my eyes with relief, and then he quietly told his story.

The two men were twins. His father Jack and his Uncle John. They were both Maori wrestlers, tribal chiefs in Rotorua and both had a huge influence on his life.

His Dad played the guitar and Uncle John taught him boxing and wrestling. In his youth Big Jim was a prize fighter. Uncle John was killed at sea. He idolised and missed them both, it was like he had two Dads.

Uncle John had no children and was a wanderer, and he'd taken Jim on many of his travels. From the age of twenty, Big Jim had been in and out of trouble with the law.

He was trying Australia as a way of escaping the past. He was alone, frightened and with no direction, his future to him looked grim.

"Please" he said "ask them, what should I do?"

I explained that they were here to reassure him, that we (earthbound souls) are never alone and that he only has to think about them and they will be by his side. If he listened carefully, he could hear the music of his Dad's guitar.

He must learn to listen, to stop, to listen to the still quiet voice and to the sounds within his body. They will come to him in his quiet moments, when he's alone. He said that was what his Dad used to say, "You never listen Jim, you always react first. You must learn to listen."

We then heard information about his daughter who was in serious trouble with drugs, and how Jim could help if he got back in touch with her. His second wife was trying to find him.

She wanted to help him too. His destiny was not here, he had to go back, stop his wandering – slow down, work through his anger and start to love himself. At which point he said: "I don't even know who I am."

Immediately the chair under me shook, I felt as though a bolt of lighting had hit me. Big Jim looked startled too. A huge voice came into my head – like a roar and I heard myself say in a voice that didn't belong to me, it felt deep and masculine;

"You are the son of a great Maori Warrior. I am of the Earth, the Sky, the Moon and the Sun. Go now and find your roots. You are my son."

That was it, there was nothing to add. Big Jim had his message and he knew what he had to do. He stood tall and walked out of the door. He seemed to have grown in that room, he hugged me like a bear – a huge teddy bear and I cried too – this time with joy in my heart. I knew that Big Jim had found his way home.

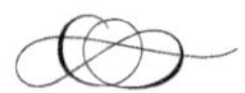

Three Internal Senses

There are three internal senses associated with psychic perception, clairvoyance, clairaudience and clairsentience.

The first level is visual perception, or the old term, clairvoyance meaning clear-vision. If you are a person with a highly developed faculty to visualise clear pictures in your mind, some of the hard work in developing your clair-vision is reduced. You perceive images with the internal eye rather like a picture on a blank screen.

We all have this ability and use it continually, for example when you are going to redecorate a room you see the finished colour scheme and soft furnishings in your mind's eye before you start.

This power to project mental images is highly developed within the clairvoyant, as if the image is outside one's head. This ability is also strongly developed in many artists.

The mental images float into the mind without the clairvoyant formulating them through thought. You just see a very clear picture.

The second level of consciousness is the clairaudience of clear-hearing. Here you are developing your ability to perceive through sounds and words.

On occasion I have noticed that when I have a picture that I do not understand, I recall the picture to gain more information and words come to me instead. This is when I know I have shifted from one level of perception that is seeing, to the perception of hearing.

The third level of consciousness is the clairsentience or clear-sensing. Again this is apparent in all of us and we use it daily. We access this part of ourselves when we sense things about people we meet for the first time, or when we walk into a room and sense a weird atmosphere.

This is highly developed in the clairvoyant and is used to give information on a person's personality, emotions and attitudes. It is perceiving through feelings.

Let's remember, tradition maintains that there is but one psychic sense of perception. These three levels of consciousness are modifications of the one basic psychic perception. Each of these levels of consciousness are therefore within all of us. We just choose to develop them or not.

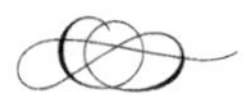

Bricks, Bricks and More Bricks

When I look back over the years I smile inwardly at the naivety with which I started this work. I was so green it was embarrassing. I truly believe that you only do things when you are ready, but this was blind ignorance.

All sorts of people have found their way to our home. The phone has never stopped ringing and my husband Colin would tell people I was no longer married to him but to a phone. People would ring at the most inappropriate times.

It eventually became necessary for me to find an office to work from. I decided that if this was the right thing to do, then Universal Energy would find me one.

True to form in January 1993 I was offered the use of some rooms in Perth. In addition someone took all my phone bookings. It was bliss, I got back my home life!

Another aspect of this work I wasn't prepared for was dealing with the general public. Not only do you need the patience of Job, you also have to be a born diplomat. In the short time people spend with you, you often touch on things in their life that are really intimate.

They leave and you may never see them again. However in April '93 I had a very amusing experience with a woman who visited me in my new office.

She arrived late and was very flustered. It seemed appropriate to spend a few moments talking to her whilst she calmed down and relaxed. I remember trying to listen within, but I was not hearing any information.

I was only receiving pictures, just like a television set. How could I tell her that all I could see were bricks, bricks and more bricks – just hundred of bricks!

What on earth is she up to? She didn't look like a builder's labourer. In fact she looked totally exhausted to me so I stopped in mid–sentence and waited for inspiration.

I heard myself say, "Bricks, what the heck?" Then the penny dropped of course. "Oh you are building a house with pale bricks. They look like crusty bricks to me, handmade ones."

"Good, good", she said "Yes, you see the house we want to build, soon I hope. Can you see the land?"

"No, you have the land already."

"Yes, that is correct."

"You will build this house before September."

"How can we, we don't have a builder."

"Well go and get one then," I said.

"Tell me, is it going to be a big house? Has it a tin roof, how many bedrooms, what about tiles and the bathrooms? How many?"

"Well it looks large."

"How many people are living in it?"

I felt like saying an army. I was getting fed up with the barrage of questions.

"Two people and one who keeps coming and going." By now I was feeling very confused. "Leaving, who's leaving? Can you see who?"

"I didn't say leaving, I said coming and going. That means they're not always there."

"Oh! Well it must be either my son or daughter. Perhaps they're getting married?"

"Your daughter is going to Queensland."

"What!" she screamed. "When, how, what for?" God, where did that come from, I thought. Here was very possessive mother who wouldn't let go of her offspring.

Diplomacy was the order of the day, "Please Spirit, do not give me anything that is going to offend this lady."

She was sitting on the edge of her chair, almost sitting on my knee. I went back to safe ground. "The house, you will have difficulties choosing the house."

"Why, what will happen? Is the builder going to overcharge us?"

"No." Dash, what can I say to her? "Well it looks like the bricks."

"What do you mean the bricks? How can we have problems with bricks?"

I wanted to shout, "I don't know," but the damn bricks are the problem. I sat like a lady and smiled sweetly (my mother would have been proud of me), and said "Well maybe they will be late in arriving or something."

She relaxed. Good, I thought. Now Spirit give me something pleasant to tell her. Wham.

"Your daughter, she is in an odd relationship?" She was at my throat again.

"Yes, she is. Can you see her getting out of it?"

"Yes, I can. He is not right for her, but they don't appear to live together do they?"

"No, she lives with me."

'Gawd', I thought, 'the daughter would be better off with the guy.'

"She's not leaving is she? We need a mortgage and she works for a Bank. She is the only one of the three of us who can get the money, you can see the money can't you?"

Worry, worry, worry. She was back worrying, I really wanted her to go.

'Please God help'. I know, I'll throw love out to her, maybe that will do the trick. I sat in silence for a moment.

I said, "Let's tune in, please, just close your eyes."

We both sat with our eyes closed whilst I sat there thinking, 'love, love' but not actually feeling it. In some book I had read, it said you only have to think love and that was enough… 'Ommmmm, Ommmmm, Loooooove, beam me up Scotty and get me out of this.'

Then suddenly I heard myself talking at a hundred miles an hour.

"You will have problems with the builder. It is something to do with the bricks, it looks like major problems with the garage door or the walls. There will be papers and many documents.

There will be a delay getting into the house that you will complete in September, but not move into until late October. The money will be fine, your daughter is going to move away, your son will change his job. I have another person waiting outside. You must go now."

I got up, took her by the hand and led her out of the door. She did not utter a word and I looked straight ahead. I knew that if our eyes met, I was done for.

Several weeks later the 'Brick Lady' came back. Jesus, Mary and Joseph and all the Blessed Saints, what are you doing to me Spirit? Do I owe this person something?

Under her arm were large scrolls of paper, which she hurriedly placed in front of me and asked "which house can you see?"

"Is this for real? Does she really expect me to identify the house?"

"But," I said, "these are just plans, there is no colour." Gawd, I sounded just like her.

"Look, look and see which is the house, then we won't take that one, that way we can avoid the problem with the builder."

"I can't see the house, I can only see cream crusty bricks – they look hand made."

This was beginning to be a joke, it sounded like the house that Jack built. Is this some trick that Spirit is playing on me?

I flippantly said: "You'll have to bring me drawings. I'm no good on plans." Then I realised that I had to pick the house as this person was unable to make decisions, I said, "Oh this house." And pointed to the one in the middle.

"Good, we won't have that one."

Off she went, as happy as a sand boy and waved a cheery goodbye. I said a few Hail Mary's, breathed a sigh of relief, laughed inwardly to myself and promptly forgot all about it.

Over the following months, news of the house filtered through. The house was completed in September and I was dutifully informed that I was wrong. Ummm, Ummm, I thought – we haven't finished yet. Sure enough she was back! Angry and flustered, with steam coming out of her nostrils.

"That builder! You were right. The stupid man used all the hand made house bricks on the inside of the garage. We only ordered enough to do the outside and he was supposed to leave the breeze blocks exposed."

"The garage door won't fit and we can't purchase any more of the hand made bricks as they are not firing that batch until next year. We are refusing to pay the last installment until the builder rectifies the situation. He claims he is going to take us to court – what can you see?"

'No more bricks,' I said.

'That's right. We won't be able to move in until November."

Spirit was tapping me on the shoulder and the voice said: 'that's what happens when you think you can outwit fate.' The Brick Lady went to court and won her case, but unfortunately put herself through a great deal of stress.

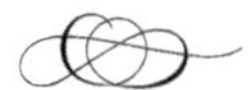

Band Aides

The moral of the story is; beware using this psychic phenomenon to make major decisions. It acts as a guide, like a road map. It can show you some pitfalls which in turn can help you handle difficult situations. However, you need to be able to change your thinking in order to turn a disaster into a positive outcome.

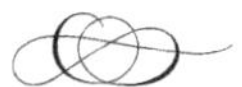

Don't Assume

As my clairvoyant ability developed, I began to understand the internal dialogue, the floating images and the physical sensations, that I experienced during a reading.

I also realised that you did not need to meet the client face to face in order to complete a reading. You could access information from a distance.

All I needed was the person's name and date of birth.

I noticed that when I concentrated on my breathing and learnt to totally relax, all I had to do was focus on the absent person's name. Information would then come into my mind regarding the person.

When I explored the possibility of remote psychic information being transmitted, I decide to start doing postal and telephone readings. I must admit the idea of readings by post frightened me as much as my early beginnings.

Here I was breaking new ground again. What if it was wrong? What an idiot I would appear.

How will I do this? Who is interested anyway? All these questions I put to myself. Doubt is the very devil itself and as usual, all I had to do was trust and wait for the right opportunity to present itself. It happened of course, but it was not what I expected.

Anna was an old friend, she rang me and asked me to do a reading for her. I was reluctant as I knew so much about her life, including her father being seriously ill.

Perhaps Anna was hoping for positive news. It is difficult to do a reading for close friends as I feel that I could cloud the reading with my own logic I always avoid it where possible.

I declined and gave her names and phone numbers of a couple of other clairvoyants. Then I felt awful as she had been so kind to me.

It was the least I could do to repay her friendship, so I decided to do a postal reading alone without Anna and talk straight into the tape recorder.

I sat and mediated to clear my own thoughts and asked Spirit to help me. When my energy felt right, I began. I turned the tape on and away I went at a hundred miles an hour.

The first major event that came into mind was associated with the death in her family in August and I felt a very heavy energy about this situation. Normally I am reluctant to verbalise this type of information as I don't want to be the bearer of bad tidings.

However, in this situation it was different as Anna's father was in and out of hospital. I felt perhaps the information would help Anna to accept her father's health condition. I knew her stepmother was not helping and that Anna was supporting her father almost single-handedly.

Associated with death, I saw a very angry man. He looked dark and seemed overweight. He was very aggressive. He was shouting at Anna about money and furniture. Again because of what I knew, I assumed he was Anna's brother although I didn't say this on the tape.

I then went on to talk about Peter, Anna's son, and his school work and the decisions he had to make. Three choices of career, forms, forms and more forms.

There was information about Anna's relationship, changes in the New Year and a commitment from her, to the man in her life. There was much more on a personal note. I popped the tape into an envelope and posted it off to her. It was June 1995.

I didn't hear from her for a few weeks except a message to say she had received the tape.

On the 31st of July, Anna's sister Lynne rang to say their stepmother Babba Yakka had died.

"What?" I screamed down the phone. "How come? My God, what a turn of events! What has happened?"

"Well the Babba Yakka went and dropped dead, just like that."

"But she was only in her fifties and there was nothing wrong with her." I said.

"Well there is now, she's dead." There was no emotion in her voice.

Babba Yakka is Polish for Witch. This was the name the two sisters had dubbed their father's second wife. Both sisters felt no affection for their stepmother as she had led their father a merry dance.

She was twenty years younger than Mr Walenska and refused to take care of him properly in his old age.

The father was back in hospital and was devastated with the news of his wife's death. Babba Yakka had an obnoxious son whom both girls had not seen for several years.

The stepson was screaming for money that he felt was his by inheritance. He was hurling abuse and obscenities at Anna, who was busy shielding her father and trying to protect his estate.

The stepson knew there was money in the family and was 'going for the jugular' and frightening the old man. He was demanding the furniture, saying that his mother had paid for it with a recent inheritance of her own and that the furniture was rightfully his.

Also he was demanding to know what had happened to all her money?

The son didn't realise that his mother had not left a will – she was expecting to outlive her husband. In fact she had talked about it quite openly on many occasions. In practice, what remained of her estate, by law, went to her next of kin, the husband.

To comfort and support their father, Lynne and Anna attended Babba Yakka's funeral. There was no feeling of loss or remorse from the two sisters – only a sense of relief that they could now take care of their father in peace.

All funerals have a format and the priest had said the eulogy so many times, he could no doubt have said it in his sleep. In fact the girls were beginning to think this was what he was doing when suddenly the priest paused, let out an almighty sneeze and spat out his set of false teeth.

They plopped straight into his quickly outstretched hand and without losing a breath, he popped them straight back in his mouth and continued the sermon, as if it was part of the routine. Lynne knew that one look in Anna's direction would set her off into fits of laughter.

Between the sisters, the father's estate was saved. Mr Walenska's health improved and he now lives in a nursing home, just a short walk from Anna's home.

It was not until after the funeral that Anna remembered the tape. She played it back and sure enough was able to piece the story and the information together. It wasn't the death we all assumed, nor Anna's own brother, who caused the distress. The information was there. We, as usual had to wait for the events to play out before the true meaning of the reading fell into place.

The moral of the story is, don't assume – it makes an ass out of you and me!

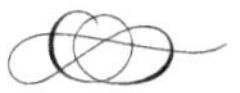

The Fourth Dimension

The fourth level of development is beyond the psyche, it is the mindset, which allows you clear perceptions of people who were once alive.

You perceive beyond the 'feeling sense' to the 'knowing sense', you neither see nor feel, you just know.

It's almost as if you are receiving information through your body. You sense the person who has passed away as if they are in the room.

You feel their personality, shape and size. You then hear information on how they entered the spirit realm.

On occasions names will be given and also quite detailed information on the person's life. Sometimes messages can be given for loved ones who are grieving.

As you work with this energy field, your internal senses move from the Spirit person then back to yourself. While this form of communication is very simple or basic, it does however help us to answer the question, is their life after death? I believe there is.

I call it the fourth dimension, the consciousness beyond thought. The form and shape is lightness and brightness, the energy that is emitted is pure love, compassion and peace.

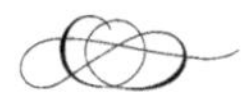

Mr Lee Lou Li

I have been so fortunate. My work has introduced me to some incredible people whether they be ordinary or extraordinary people. Of all the people I have worked with, I have special admiration for those who have endured horrendous experiences without complaint.

These people are special; their will to live is a tribute to the human race. They live their lives and often go unnoticed; they are our unsung heroes.

Through this work I have learnt so much about the human spirit, about the power within each of us to keep going forward. The human spirit is the part of us that lives forever.

It is natural for us to keep living, growing, and always going forward. How do we contact this spirit energy, this part of us that travels on and on and on? It is the intangible within us, the untouchable part, the unseen.

We see nature with our eyes, we feel Spirit Energy with our senses. It begins as an internal experience then develops through visualisation with the image becoming clearer as information about the person's life unfolds.

Eventually you perceive a whole picture and the essence of the person comes through as if they are in the room.

I was alone in our home in Melbourne the first time I experienced contact with Spirit prior to a client's visit. We hadn't been living in the house long and I thought someone was trying to break in as I heard a noise in the lounge room. I walked gingerly into the room.

He was there but he wasn't there, yes, he was sitting in the chair as large as life. I saw his feet first, small black canvas shoes with elastic sides and plain white socks, baggy black pants and the traditional black Chinese shirt.

His face was round and his eyes full of pride. He was elderly, a peaceful presence, then he was gone in a flash. My imagination is running wild I thought. I don't know many Asian people – cheeky thing sitting in my lounge as large as life.

I moved into the front bedroom and decided to strip the sheets off the bed. He was there too, sitting in the corner. "OK, who is this?" I heard myself say. I sat down to tune in.

He disappeared and I had the sensation that he was talking to me, but it was hard to hear him. He told me he was Lee Li Li. Lie on the bed I thought. Are you serious? He wants me to lie on my bed!

"No! No! My name is Lee Lou Li, I come from Vietnam." He explained that his daughter and grand daughter were coming to see me, that was why he was here, he wanted to comfort his daughter. He talked about lemons and oranges and about some land in Vietnam. He said to tell her he was still there. He disappeared again.

I sat for quite a while, tuning into his energy. I felt peaceful, quiet and extremely relaxed. I could have stayed there all day with this glorious feeling of peace. It took me ages to make the bed as I kept hearing music and high pitched singing. In the end I heard myself say, "Look you'll have to go, I have work to do."

An hour later the phone rang, it was a young girl called Tammy. She had an Asian accent and I knew who she was immediately. I said, "You'd better come early this evening." Tammy explained that it was her mother Soo Liu who wanted to come. Tammy said she would act as interpreter as her mother spoke very little English.

The ladies arrived at 7pm on the dot. I still felt calm and relaxed; I knew that my Asian gentleman was with us. I began to talk as soon as we sat down.

'Who is Mr Lee Loo Li?" I asked the mother.

Tammy using her dialect corrected the pronunciation. It sounded like a song when she spoke his name.

Soo Liu immediately became emotional.

"That was my grandfather, who died several years ago." Said Tammy. I explained that he had been with me this morning. Soo Liu was thrilled. I then went on to ask what oranges and lemons meant to them both, as they meant nothing to me.

Soo Liu was very excited, she spoke quickly and Tammy translated. Grandfather had orange trees and made his living selling the fruit, Tammy's aunt who lives in Vietnam, looks after the fruit farm now.

I felt as if Mr Lee Lou Li's spirit was inside me. He seemed to be smaller than I was, his shoulders hurt and back ached. He was showing me books, pens, papers and ink bottles.

He told me he was a man of letter that he had been outspoken and had tried to prevent the oppression of his people. He stood up for what he believed, he was an activist in his youth and fought against aggression, he was a man of honour. I repeated all this to Soo Liu and Tammy.

Tammy was able to confirm this information was correct. She went on to explain that the family had fled from Vietnam because of Mr Lee Lou Li's political activities and he had been imprisoned and tortured for his actions. The authorities had threatened to imprison the whole family and they all had to leave very quickly, they were lucky to escape with their lives.

If he had lived in a Western country he would have been honoured for his humanitarian activities. That explained the pride in his eyes and the sense of nobility he had about him.

He had come to visit me today ahead of his daughter in order to introduce himself. This was part of his culture, he was a gentleman. He wanted to remind his daughter about the religious upbringing he had taught his family.

For some reason it was necessary that she remember. The move to Australia had badly affected her two sons who were now both drug addicts, with police records.

Again I asked, 'Is this correct Tammy?"

Tammy nodded and repeated all this to her mother. Soo Liu's eyes brimmed with tears and she nodded her head. It had been a terribly hard road for Soo Liu and her family. Australia had given them opportunities for work and monetary rewards but at the cost of her sons' well being and future.

The lady was distraught. Both boys were beyond help and she was at her wit's end. She had no one to turn to as her husband had returned to Vietnam, and he had recently resumed his family's business. Soo Liu was fully occupied running their restaurant in Australia.

The father was putting pressure on the daughter to take a position in Vietnam. If the daughter went back home, Soo Liu would be all alone. The daughter was torn between two parents. The mother could also go, but the boys were in and out of prison and she would have to abandon them, which she couldn't bring herself to do.

The old man was asking the two women to pray, to ask for help from a source greater than them. The mother's face lit up and she smiled as Tammy translated. I heard my voice say, "All is well with the orange trees. Remember the red boxes and the shrine in the house? How fruit was always placed on low tables near the Buddha. Listen and you will hear the memory of the silence around the house when we worshipped Buddha.

Listen and you will hear the water on our land, you will remember the smell of the earth. Listen and you will feel the presence of Buddha."

Apparently he had pictures of Buddha in the house and always placed the fruit boxes at the base of the shrine on a low table. See Liu remembered, her face relaxed, she smiled to herself and realised it was all in Buddha's hands. There was little more she could do except give it all up to Buddha. Tammy and her mother left the room, arms around one another, with her mother saying.

'Yes, it is with Buddha, Yes it is with Buddha, Yes it is with Buddha."

I didn't see Tammy or Soo Liu again. The grandfather stayed around the house for days, moving from room to room. His nobility and pride are something we see so little of today. It is a shame we have lost so many of those beautiful and honourable values.

I can feel him standing next to me, right now. I bow to you Mr Lee Lou Li, I salute your God, your Buddha. Thank you for coming into my life.

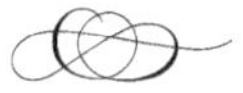

Let Go of Fear and Live

People from all walks of life, religions, creeds and beliefs have knocked on my door. Nothing surprises me anymore. At some stage in the reading Spirit will find a way of turning the focus back to basics and the meaning of existence.

There is always the time honoured question – Is there a God? We do not know the form that God takes, that is of little importance. Each and everyone of us has within us a knowing on one level or another, that there is a power, a force that protects us, guides us, evokes within us incredible sensations.

Once we wake up to our own internal understanding of this essence, our life takes on a different meaning. Life becomes an experience in Human Consciousness – a simple process if we allow it to be so!

Believe, Trust and Know your God. Let go of fear and live!

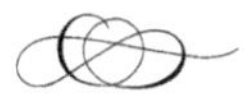

Singing for his Supper

People's lives touch you deeply in this work. One person who remained in my thoughts for weeks was Tony. He had a special energy, his charisma was infectious. His voice was deep and resonated like a cello. As he moved, his shirt rustled and his aftershave remained in the room once he had gone. He had a presence about him. Why would a man so confident visit a middle-aged clairvoyant?

It was necessary to sit in silence for several minutes, whilst I tuned in. I started using my Psyche then realised this was wrong. I waited. Poor man, he must have thought I was vacant. "Singing, you are a singer?" He was on the edge of his chair.

'Yes, yes you have it." His deep voice had connected with Spirit. Before I could go on, his father came through.

"I have a man here, he is very tall, he is asking why have you stopped singing and when do you intend to continue? He is dark, very dark, and not at all like you, Tony. He too could sing."

In fact, singing played a large part in the family's entertainment. The family felt very male and I expressed this to Tony. It seemed that his father had not always approved of him.

Tony was so different from the other son's, though he had the best voice, which his father had to acknowledge.

He was here to say sorry to his son. I detected a note of disappointment in the father's message.

Then a lady stepped forward, she was small, very dainty and she was his mother. Tony was thrilled with the connection. He loved his mother and missed her; he was overjoyed at making the contact. She too was encouraging him to continue with his singing.

There were many questions and Tony wanted answers. Both his mother and father helped and he seemed satisfied. I could see envelopes, two large yellow ones with contracts in them.

"But you cannot fulfill these contracts here; you have to go overseas to Singapore." I said.

"Yes," he said "One of these contracts was for a music score that was to be presented to a famous musical director".

He wanted to know the outcome. Both parents gave him information on the results being favourable but not with the first draft. The one that would work would be the fourth. I felt impelled to ask what he was doing in Australia, in particular Perth, and why had he left his singing career and England behind.

I said there had been many women in his life and I identified a particular situation that he was running away from. He admitted I was right.

His story began in the late sixties. He had had a brilliant career and was on the road as a support singer with Tom Jones and Englebert Humperdink. His pregnant girlfriend whom he adored and was about to marry, was also a talented entertainer.

They were driving home one night after a party when he lost control of the car on the wet road. The accident was dreadful, the car was a write-off, his fiancé and the baby was killed instantly.

He had never forgotten or forgiven himself and blamed himself for years. Nothing had helped. He left the music industry and spent many years in a total mess emotionally.

Only as a result of learning about metaphysics had he been able to piece his life back together. He had now reached the understanding that the accident was not totally his fault.

It was supposed to happen. He now had to go forward and resume his career, only this time he intended to sing from the heart and not the pocket. This time he was going to make singing his passion.

He left the room and some of his sadness stayed with me. I knew that I would hear from this man again. To have the gift of song and not use it, was to me a tragedy.

We must do something for him. I was returning to Melbourne the next day. I couldn't get this story out of my head and so I contacted another Medium who lived in Perth.

I asked her if she could see Tony. As we chatted over the phone, she suddenly said, "Ring him, tell him to come this week. I have a young woman here; she has a baby in her arms. It is his there is a message for him." I had not told Chris, Tony's story. She was tuning in directly to Spirit.

Again a new experience for me, a realisation that we were both tapping into the same energy. We both had contact with the Spirit world at the same time. I was so excited, here we were hundreds of miles apart and over the telephone, Chris and I were both receiving the same pictures, sounds and information.

This is how collective consciousness works, it is amazing. Spirit will, and can bridge the gap and this was a classic example of the workings of Spirit. We were both used as conduits of sound and light to transfer a message to an Earth Soul who was in need of help. I had felt compelled to take action. Something inside me was pushing me.

I knew that a further message for this man had to be transmitted, that I had not received the final message; it was to be delivered through the second medium. There had to be a reason for this, time would reveal the answer.

Although it was difficult to locate Tony, we eventually did. The visit to the Perth medium was highly successful and Tony's healing is well underway. His second message helped him to forgive himself, accept his life and realise that peace of mind, is possible. For when our mind is settled and we are at peace with ourselves, we can go forward with our lives.

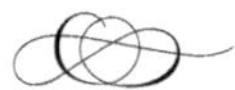

An Inspirational Moment

It is this type of experience that inspires me to continue to see, to understand this incredible phenomenon. Every day I learn a little more and every day I realise I know so little.

I sometimes feel so small, like a speck of dust in this vast ocean of learning. All I know is that I must go on.

Developing The Psyche

We understand the five physical sense as sight, sound, taste, smell and touch. The three internal senses can be developed with practice and the help of a good teacher to guide you.

It is rather like a wine taster, when he is developing his palate, or a chef when he is learning to blend flavours in new recipes. They both have to develop the physical sense of taste and can benefit from guidance in their initial development.

Learning to see pictures with inner perception is hard if you are a person who finds visualisation difficult. To overcome this I suggest you use guided meditation tapes, which give, detailed pictures to visualise as you listen. If you use the same tape over and over again, you will learn to create the pictures easily.

Another exercise is to try to see blotches of colour at the back of the retina. It is possible to do this if you relax and concentrate on colour. Simple exercises like these will help you to develop your internal eye which is the sense called clairvision. The only way you succeed at anything, is with practice.

To develop the internal perception of sound and word you have to learn to listen on a deep level. Again I would use meditation tapes, this time a tape on sound such as a mantra or toning. You need to listen to the rhythm and the beat .

Another excellent exercise is to listen to your heartbeat and also your breathing. When you concentrate on your breathing you can slow the mind. When you are able to maintain a silent mind, you are in mastery of self. Listening to silence is brilliant for developing the internal sense of clairaudience. This takes practice too.

Clairsentience is the internal sense of feeling. This is the classic and most obvious perception to develop rather like sight. We continuously use this sense, it's that 'gut' feeling. How often you hear people say "Oh, I had a feeling that would happen."

This internal sense is the easiest to develop, all you have to do is pay attention to the feelings within your body. As you start to focus on this sense of perception, write events down. When you get them right you will learn to identify the accuracy of your intuition. This is fun as you realise, "Hey, I was right." You need to consciously practice this.

Tuning in to Spirit Energy is only an extension of the three faculties, you can access this energy field through the clairsentience. You blend all three internal senses and end up with a sense of 'knowing'.

It becomes easier as you learn to trust yourself. However I would like to point out you do need a teacher to help you at this stage. I don't recommend you undertake this development on your own, as you need to be able to assess and assimilate what you are receiving.

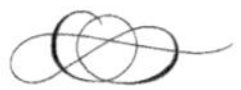

Aberdeen Street and Much More!

My journey and life experiences have introduced me to opportunities beyond my wildest dreams. Speaking to groups of people about my work has been another stage of development. I have found myself in some truly amazing situations.

One recent engagement was at a house in Perth and as I walked through the gate, I heard myself say; "Why is this place hidden between the coffee shops and the restaurants?

What a weird place for the over-sixties, to meet, right in the heart of Perth's nightlife. Oh well, it takes all sorts." My internal reply was: 'Keep an open mind Pam and just do what you are told!' That bossy Spirit person was around again, I could feel it. How I wish I could catch this elusive energy that skips around me!

I was right on time. The house was old, very old, a period piece, restored not by tender loving care, but more out of total necessity. I opened the door and took a step back. The walls were covered with posters on Aids, Menopause, Cervical Cancer, Breast Tests, PMT and numerous other female ailments. "Is this 100 Aberdeen Street?" I asked the lady who approached me.

"Yes, that's right, we are a Women's Health Centre."

"Oh" I blinked twice and cleared my throat. "Humm, but I have come to speak to a women's group, called OWN."

"O.K. Spirit, is this some kind of a joke? Am I supposed to find twenty women here, in their 60's?" It looks too official for a social group to meet here. What, pray, is this big idea of yours?"

"Yes, you are in the right place," replied the polite office receptionist.

Whoops, I wondered if she'd heard my thoughts!

Then a door opened and out popped a cheery lady in her mid-sixties. She grabbed my hand and whisked me through the door. I found myself amidst a group of ladies who were sitting in a circle around the perimeter of the room. I was positioned right in the middle. These ladies varied in age, the youngest being a spritely sixty!

I gulped and heard myself say, "Please could you tell me something about your group." Thinking this would buy me time whilst I worked out what the heck to say next.

'Jesus, Mary and Joseph and all the blessed Saints…Help!!! Come quick and bring reinforcements."

I didn't have a chance to collect my thoughts as their story was riveting. They were excitedly telling me about the house, it was originally Perth's most famous brothel. The ladies of the night had serviced the male sex, right through two world wars. This house of ill repute had closed its doors to the profession about six years ago. The room we were sitting in, was the ladies' parlour, where they entertained their men.

The ladies all giggled mischievously at the thought of all the antics which these walls had witnessed. The group had tried on several occasions to find more appropriate rooms to hold their weekly meetings, but each time they returned to this parlour.

They all agreed they were drawn to the place. Someone said, "Perhaps we were ladies of the night in a previous life. Can you see for us, Pam?"

'Heaven forbid' I thought 'what was I supposed to see? Naughty nighties and lovers by the score?' I didn't feel inclined to look behind *that* door. I declined and gave my sauciest wink, which seemed to satisfy the inquirer.

The Centre had been established four years ago and served as an information place for sexually transmitted diseases. Again, they all giggled. I didn't see the humour, I saw the balance of life and the excess of the past being rectified by treatment methods of the present.

There is justice in the world after all.

Although the house had sadness within its walls, this room felt warm and welcoming. It had incredible vibes and I could hear the echo of laughter and music. This was indeed the room for entertainment.

It seemed appropriate to me that this group met here just to socialise. As I looked around the room lives flashed past me, lives of heartache, suffering and loss, laughter at the fall of fate, loves lost, fortunes made and stolen.

Life is funnier than fiction and true to style, up popped Spirit to set the scene of merriment. As I touched one lady's hand, saw her house and the room she worked in – all her arts and crafts and the kitchen. She had just bought herself a new cheese grater and I heard myself telling her this. The woman nodded and the whole room collapsed into fits of laughter. Of all the things to tune in to first, a blooming cheese grater!

This was Spirit, having fun. The next lady was chortling to herself when I heard about a script she was rewriting and promptly told her, it would work. Apparently she was applying for a grant from her local repertory company. She was thrilled to bits but looked most sceptically at me.

I then turned right around to face a tall, slim lady. Whoops, here comes Spirit. I felt this energy bigger than me. Sure enough, it was a man.

"Who is the elderly man you knew, who is now in spirit? He had a walking stick and smells of pipe tobacco, he has his hand over his eye."

I continued. "He felt like a miserable old so and so, a right problem. He is telling me you must keep the house."

The woman roared "My God, that's my father-in-law Jack. He was a right old misery guts, he lost an eye in the war."

"Quick," she said, "what's he telling you about the house?"

"Well, just to keep it, not to let it go."

"Good," she said, "ask him some more."

"Well, he says that's all and he was sorry he was such a 'pain in the neck' and thank you for being so good to him."

"So he should," said the lady. "I was the only one who looked after him and he was not even my Dad. The house is mine and my son wants to buy it off me. He has been pestering me for months, but I won't sell it now. Will you thank Jack for me?"

I duly said. "Did you hear that? She said thanks?" The room erupted in laughter, Spirit was on form today. The next lady was quietly taking it all in and saying nothing. She was elegant and obviously had looked after herself. I turned to hold her hand and someone said;

"Nancy is ninety two, she is the oldest of us." I wanted to say the brightest too, but kept my thoughts to myself.

Into the room came two ladies from Spirit, one had blonde hair, the second one was large.

"Excuse me, but do you have two sisters in Spirit?"

"Yes, I do." She replied.

"Well, they are both here, standing next to me." Her eyes opened as big as saucers. "One is telling me, she wished she had been you, that you kept telling them how to look after themselves, but they didn't listen."

'Yes, that's right." She said. "They were silly women, they let their men walk all over them. I said it would be the death of them and it was.

They should have been like me, I told them and I told them. I had three husbands and each one left me better off than the last. You have to treat men hard and keep them keen. Not those two, they were soft alright."

Beryl, the spokeswoman turned to me and asked if I could help the lady sitting near the door. I moved over to her, she needed healing, her health seemed poor. I asked her if she had problems with her knees, she nodded her head. I placed my hands on her knees and they soaked up the heat in my hands. She smiled, but she had the saddest eyes.

"Wow" I said "I see hats with you and hat pins and hat stands." She explained that she had a milliner's shop for years and made hats for a living.

I could see her granddaughter, she was about twelve, "She's artistic too." She explained she was teaching her to sew.

I waited, Spirit did not transmit. I just heard information about her son. "You have a son with problems?"

"Yes," she replied. "Can you help me please? I have been praying and praying for God to help me. My son has removed himself from my life and will not have anything to do with me. I don't understand why. He wouldn't come to my 80th birthday and he will not explain what's wrong. My daughter-in-law comes to see me, but not him."

"Oh no" the voice in my head said "The family is splitting up. What do I say?" I heard myself say "Your son will come back to you, once he has sorted out his differences with his wife.

He will visit you again with his daughter, without his wife." I looked deep into her eyes and held her gaze for what seemed an eternity. I stayed by her side, she understood. Her eyes filled with tears. There was nothing else to say.

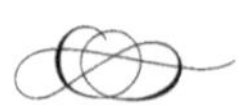

Ladies in Waiting

What a wonderful morning we had, sharing stories of our lives together, laughing at ourselves and receiving delightful messages from Spirit. That there is life after life, we all agreed. These ladies were very much alive and full of fun. I revisited them in December. To their delight, some of the predictions had already happened and other events were still waiting to unfold.

I have learnt to trust Spirit to take me where I need to be. I now put my life in the hands of an energy greater than mine. Living this way has brought miracles into my life.

To me miracles are anything or events that turn out to be better than I anticipated. Miracles happen daily. Visiting Aberdeen Street was an experience that I would not have missed for the world!

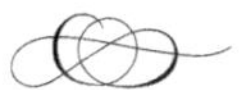

Loves Lost

It's always hard when you're giving a talk in public, to keep the atmosphere light and happy. When you are working with Spirit you do not always know what will happen next. You have to be prepared to work through situations with grace and ease, as you can upset your energy field. This in turn can break the link with Spirit.

On one such occasion in Melbourne, at a View Club Function, I found myself placing my hand on a lady's back and I heard myself say, "I have to come round to the front of you, I have to see your face." All I could hear was 'son', that there was A message from her son. I then felt totally cold and this huge feeling of trauma came over me.

"Your son, we have to talk about your son." 'Dear God help me.' A chill ran down my spine as I realised he was in Spirit. I have started this now, I have to finish it. I stayed calm, I waited and looked straight at the lady's face.

"Please everybody, help us here." I heard myself say to the lady. "Help your son, pray for him please. There is sadness within him." The group fell silent, then the lady slowly spoke.

"My son died twelve months ago today. That is why I am here, he was nineteen and I wasn't with him when he died. I can't forgive myself that I didn't say goodbye. This group of people has helped me so much, through these last months.

Today I learnt from the doctor that my son died of a heart condition, that his heart burst a huge blood vessel. I was unaware that he had has a heart condition from birth. I miss him so."

"He is asking you to pray for him. He is sending you all his love." The lump in my throat was huge, it took me all my energy to stay calm.

Each one of us sitting near her, placed our hands on her shoulders and we all sat in silence and prayed for the mother and son. Those of us with sons and daughters felt her pain, we couldn't take the pain away, but we could give hope to those who were suffering.

On occasions it is necessary for Spirit to bring forth this reaction within me, so I feel the depth of compassion that Spirit has for us, mortal beings. The feeling defies description in words.

It must be amazing to those on the other side, working with those of us in this dimension, when they actually make contact and we get it right! I wonder if they applaud our success?

Sometimes you actually miss things that are really important and later you find yourself saying…"Oh, I heard that this morning, why didn't I listen?"

One such example was on a recent visit to Rockingham Ladies Circle. I was busy trying to navigate using a map. Not one of my best skills, I never did work out the right and left thing.

A voice in my head said, "Hello, it's Jim Tapley here." 'Oh, yes,' I thought 'Spirit was here already.' "Look Jim, just give me a chance to get to this meeting. Clear off for a minute, I really need to concentrate."

By this time, I had a clear picture of an elderly man, sitting in the front seat. "O.K. so you're here to help navigate, right? I get the message, you're here to make sure I get there. Yep." It was someone's husband and he wanted to make contact.

The meeting had already started when I arrived. The President of the club was in full flow and was very entertaining. I remember thinking, 'Gawd what a hard act to follow.' As I looked around the room, I realised several of the ladies were knitting! Knitting in a fund raising group. Well, I suppose some women are superwomen and can listen and knit at the same time.'

Before I knew what had hit me, I was up standing next to the President and being introduced. It was pointed out that although these ladies were retired, they were rather hoping that I could "spook" things up a bit! I did a mental somersault and thought I should have brought my devils' horns and tail!

I quickly realised that with sixty people in the room, the wires could easily get crossed, so asked for volunteers. A bad idea! Everyone who could raise a hand did. So I chose four ladies. The first lady was difficult. The information didn't fit. I knew it belonged to someone in the room but didn't feel inclined to stay with it.

I moved up and down the aisle, working away. I found myself standing next to a lady in a green shirt, holding her watch. All of a sudden, I said " I have to talk to you on your own, later. Please do not leave until we have spoken. I have a message for you."

The morning closed and the ladies were not "too spooked." Someone approached me and explained that the first information I gave out was for her, and that It was spot on, right to the description of her mum, her sister and her mother's bad health.

As I turned to leave, the lady in the green, was by my side. She introduced herself as Joan. I had forgotten that I'd asked her to stay.

"Oh, yes, that's right, a message. John, Jim a name T T T?"

"It's my husband, he was John Taggorty. He died last June." Explained Joan.

With that we were off like a rocket. Out flew the information, at a hundred miles an hour. Her house, the orchids, his son, his tools in the shed, the new bedroom, and how she loved it, her trip to England – the whole gamut came rushing out. He then gave her some future predictions that Joan was thrilled about.

We both had a ball, talking with the husband and making the contact. He was a terrific man, a really good communicator.

As I got in the car to drive home, the voice in my head said, "If you'd listened this morning, you'd have got it right the first time. See, I was John Taggorty not Jim Tapley. I told you, but you were too busy as usual!"

I replied "Do you mean to tell me that I went all the way down to Rockingham, just to meet your wife?"

"That's right, and guess what? You'd better learn how to get there cos' you'll be going back again."

As John predicted, the phone ran hot with bookings for many full days work, in Rockingham. And I did get a better road map! You see, when you work with Spirit, it will take you where you need to be.

All you have to do is trust and go with the flow!

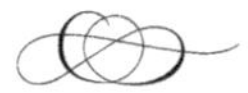

Are You Serious?

In closing, I would like to share with you, one hilarious story that always leaves me wondering if I was the victim of a practical joke.

You sometimes get the daftest questions, when deep in the middle of a riveting bit of information that you are transmitting, a person will say: "Oh! I have one really important question that I must ask."

"What, what?" you hold your breath, waiting for something deep and meaningful.

"I lost my bracelet last year. Can you see it?"

I must add, some clairvoyants are brilliant in finding missing things, unfortunately I am not one.

Or, you get a phone call, at quarter to midnight. You jump out of bed, thinking, it's an international family call. You hear "Ummm, I came to you for a reading in January and you said I would receive some excellent news on August 10. Well, I've waited all day for it, nothing has happened." You feel like shouting down the phone, "P..s off, it's midnight."

People continually ask for lotto numbers and will also ring up to check whether I can see them winning this week! It really is amazing. Photos are handed to you of lovers who have moved on some years since and the person wants to know if the guy still loves them.

One 'fruit and nut' case who came to see me, really freaked me out. He came to tell me he was the keeper of crystals and that he was on a mission to save all the crystals in the world. I tried to take him seriously. I nearly wet myself at the thought of this poor little man, pulling a trailer full of the crystals in the hereafter. Lordy lordy, couldn't you just imagine it ? And he was no bigger than a pencil sharpener!

He also informed me that he had come to introduce me to his guide. Wow! I thought, now this should be entertaining. What sort of person is guiding someone as big as a pencil sharpener?

He took out his prayer mat and settled himself on the floor cross legged, did the obligatory Omms, Umms and Satnams and then began. I waited with baited breath. I was convinced by this time to expect a crystal of magnificent proportions to materialise, vis a vis Sai Baba.

His stomach muscles did the most incredible things. They gyrated beneath his ribs, then from somewhere deep inside him, probably his bowel, came the most incredible belch, followed by a series of burps.

Ali Baba! I thought, this is how you bring up flatulence through your mouth! Trying not to explode into fits of laughter, I silently rocked on my chair, holding my stomach. The burps, and belches continued. I got up to open the door. Enough is enough, I was out of here. As I moved, pencil sharpener came out of his trance to ask what I thought of "his infiniteness, his guide."

'Hmmm," said I, "How long have you been communicating in this manner with Gases?"

"Gases, Gases Oh! You heard his name, thank you, thank you, it is Gases! I never knew his name. I can't thank you enough."

Off he popped, as quick as he came, chanting "Gases, Gases you came…!' I was left with my mouth open, unable to speak. This 'new age' movement has a lot to answer for. All I had done, was add a bit more!

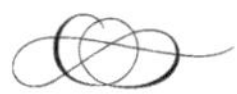

The Magic of Working With Spirit

Through my journey into the realms of mind energy, the psyche and communication with Spirit energy, I have come to many bridges, crossroads, valleys and huge mountains, all of which I feel I have climbed. The internal journey is as difficult as any Outward Bound adventure. Perhaps more so as you have no road map or compass, 'only pictures and this voice in your head'.

There is a dimension beyond life that exists in a form that we mortals cannot comprehend. Those of us who are sensitive to these different perceptions of sight and sound, do not doubt it. We know of its existence. Once more of us choose to work in this field, we will open up the conscious minds of even more people and make them aware of this phenomenon.

We are slowly embracing the challenge with positive results. More and more people are becoming involved in Metaphysics – which is wonderful. We mortals are so frightened by the unknown. We usually need to have concrete evidence before we will accept a concept.

The Spirit world will continue to contact us until the day we acknowledge its existence as a reality. That day will be a breakthrough in man's evolution. Then death will no longer be feared and life will take on a new meaning. For living is experiencing, all the trauma, disasters, grief, sadness, joys, romances, enjoyment and laughter that you wish to embrace in your personal journey.

Allowing the wonderful world of Spirit into your life introduces you to a dimension beyond the physical. All you really have to do is allow yourself to be used as a transmitter. If you're full of fear and think something or someone is going to take you 'over', you won't be successful. You are in control, you can switch it on or off just like a telephone.

Keeping an open mind is very important. Trusting the information is accurate is a challenge to begin with. As you accept the process you realise how easy it actually is.

It is my belief that this phenomenon is a very simple or basic form of communication and it is important that this form of communication is further developed.

There is a need and a reason for this phenomenon which, as yet, we are still trying to understand.

Man has the ability to do and achieve anything he or she desires, why not develop this too!

There are benefits for each of us, to use our intuition in our daily lives, you learn to slow down, you learn that everything has a time frame.

It stops you rushing your life away. It teaches you patience, peace of mind and brings balance into your life.

You then find yourself really enjoying every day as a new adventure. Simple things become luxuries, as you start to just enjoy all and everything in your life.

Through my work with Spirit I have learnt that people are very special and each of us needs to be treated with great care. Our time on this planet is so short, let's rejoice in the miracle of being alive.

P.S. Through the work I do, I have met some amazing people. To all those who have touched my life, I say thank you.

"To have the ability to laugh at yourself, is for me, the greatest gift of all."

Keep laughing, keep smiling, and to all those dear friends who have helped me with this book, I thank you for being in my life.

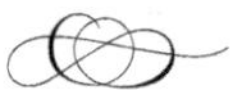

Pam Bradbury
Clairvoyant Medium

PUBLIC SPEAKING ENGAGEMENTS

Pam is an experienced Public Speaker with a charisma that enthralls all her audiences. Her information on the psyche and the spirit world is riveting. In her talks Pam shares with you her humorous stories gained from past experiences. She draws on the audience to bring forth information through her clairvoyant ability.

TOPICS INCLUDE:

- HOW THE PSYCHE WORKS
- CONNECTING WITH SPIRIT
- THE HEALING POWER WITHIN

In each topic Pam will demonstrate her clairvoyant and mediumistic abilities in a light-hearted and open manner.

PRIVATE READINGS

Pam is available for private readings. Her readings take 45 minutes; they are recorded for you to listen to, at your leisure. Relationships, family, finance, health and career are but a few of the areas she helps you with. Pam will also link you with members of your family, in spirit, if it is appropriate.

For further information please visit Pam's website: www.pambradbury.com.au

TELEPHONE SESSONS

Telephone Sessions and Skype Calls: Pam connects with clients over the telephone and with Skype from all corners of the globe. Her 30 mins readings are recorded for you and sent to a website to collect or posted to your address. Her Skype nos is: Pamela.Bradbury58.

MATERIALS AVAILABLE FROM PAM BRADBURY INCLUDE:

E/Newsletter:

Pam Bradbury produces an email newsletter on techniques you can use from your own psychic and personal development. Help on how you to turn your dreams into reality are given in the newsletter together with news of her courses and workshops.

How to access the Psyche

This is a practical booklet of exercises. Each exercise is designed to help you develop your psyche. These exercises can be used on your own or in a group situation.

They are simple and include:

- How to use visualisation in order to access the Clairvoyant vision
- Meditation techniques for developing the Clairaudio faculty
- Simple methods of how to use the Clairsentience

Visit the Products Page at: www.pambradbury.com.au

MEDITATION CDs

Creative Harmony

This is a meditation CD to assist you in creating a positive mind set.

The benefits from this tape are that you will be able to balance your conscious mind, your subconscious mind with the higher conscious mind. When you learn to focus these three mind sets into one, you have accessed this divine mind.

Healing Light

This is a creative visualization CD with light beams of healing entering your body to clear and focus you mind into optimum health.

Both CDs are suitable for individuals or group work. Demonstrations samples are on the product page of the website.

SIMPLY ORDER BY VISITING: www.pambradbury.com.au

Testimonials

"I would like to thankyou for that reading you gave me, I was 17 at the time. I am now 27 these are things you told me back then. I would move to Melbourne. I would be involved in teaching or lecturing adults. I would travel to North America and live there. I would do extensive study. Plus you said I would write a book. All of the above happened and I am currently working on my PhD which I hope to turn into a book one day. I am blown away with your accuracy even today."

Sarah Pegrum (Perth) Canada.

"Pam connects to a depth that I have never yet experienced – thoughts that have been held "deep" and for many, many years are bought to the forefront and the unexplained becomes very clear. Pam has a very special gift which she uses with great respect and a in a very positive manner. An hour with Pam gave me a deeper understanding of those in my life, both here in the present and those that have passed on. This gave me both the courage and foresight to move forward, thank you lovely lady."

Liz McMahon, Brisbane.

"The first time I met Pam Bradbury the depth of detail was so explicit it was bewildering. Names and facts were recounted that were only specific to me, and in many instances, only known by me! Pam has predicted my moving house before it's even been on my radar, provided timely career advice, cautioned me about the precise health issues of loved ones and more recently foreseen my move to Paris for work – It happened I live there now.
Over the years I have been happy to send many friends to Pam and without exception all have had amazingly positive – and uncannily accurate – experiences. As far as I'm concerned, Pam is the real deal wrapped up in an engaging and compassionate package!"

Alexandra Bergstrom, Paris, France.

"From the moment I sat down Pam did all the talking no open ended questions to fish for clues to give me bogus reading this was the most accurate and thorough reading I have ever had. I would recommend Pam to anyone looking for guidance into the spiritual world."
Shannon Cummins, Longhorn Ranch Bargo.

"About 30 seconds after I got off the phone from you I had another look at my piece of paper I scribbled a few things on. I saw the name 'Christine' and for some reason my sister-in-law popped into my head as we were speaking. Then you asked about another person dying within a year or so of my Gran and I went completely blank. Maybe it's the 'speed-thinking-under-pressure' thing. You think so hard you miss the obvious. In the little village I grew up in the mother of one of my friends was like a mam to me. I loved her dearly and she passed away 2 years ago now — her name was Christine — and I mourned her passing as if she had been my blood-mother. I don't know how I could have forgotten — it was such a powerful experience for me."

Sharon McGlinchey, NSW.

"Just wanted to say a big thank you for the reading you gave me last November. In the reading you mentioned that I should get my kidney/ ovarian area checked out. I have seen a doctor and got a referral for scans and they found several cysts and a thickening of the uterus. The cyst causing concern is adjacent to the ovary and I suspect the Doctor will need to do further tests to determine the course of treatment. Hopefully all will be Ok. I had noticed very recently some minor changes to my cycle, however without the reading I would have taken a wait and see approach."

Julie Davenport, NSW.

"I was desperate. I rang Pam for a telephone reading and over the phone she described my ex-husband, the situation with my divorce and then proceeded to tell me that I would win in the end. She even gave me a date. April 9th. I was skeptical right up to the day of the court date. I still did not believe her. Then is happened the children were given back to me with no issues hanging over our life style. It was a dream come true. Thank you Pam for being there for me. Hurray for 9th April."

Bonny Davis, Queensland.

"I was hunting for commercial office space. I enlisted Pam's Psychic insights. She actually came with me and within four hours of using her methods I had found my divinely right commercial factory for my perfumes. I recommend Pam to anyone who is going around in circles. Focus and go for it is her motto. Many Thanks Pam."

Karen Price Franke, Dubai.

"Only I knew that my son had been buried in a dinner suit and fabulous white shirt. Pam told me this information as I entered her rooms. This was such a joy to hear and gave me so much comfort to know that we had an immediate connection with my darling son in the spirit world. Thank you Pam".

Yvonne, Sydney.

"At a recent visit with Pam my daughter who had died in an accident started to give Pam information about forth coming events in the Victoria & Queensland areas. She mentioned floods and a serious fire. She said a well known Melbourne celebrity would be affected by these fires. This was early in February 09. Then the Melbourne fires happened. Both Pam and I were shocked when we realized that my daughter in the spirit world had told us this in advance. Keep up the work Pam."

Claudette, Mosman.

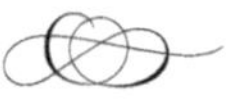